# Sampung Mga Daliri
## Ten Little Fingers

adapted by Adriana Allen
illustrated by Raquel Li

Hi!

I'm Chloe, and am proud to be a Filipino-American! Come join me around New York City as I learn how to say different body parts and actions in Tagalog by singing the traditional folk song, Sampung Mga Daliri.

:)

NYC street graffiti

Sampung mga daliri

*(sum-pung mah-ngah dah-lee-ree)*

Ten little fingers

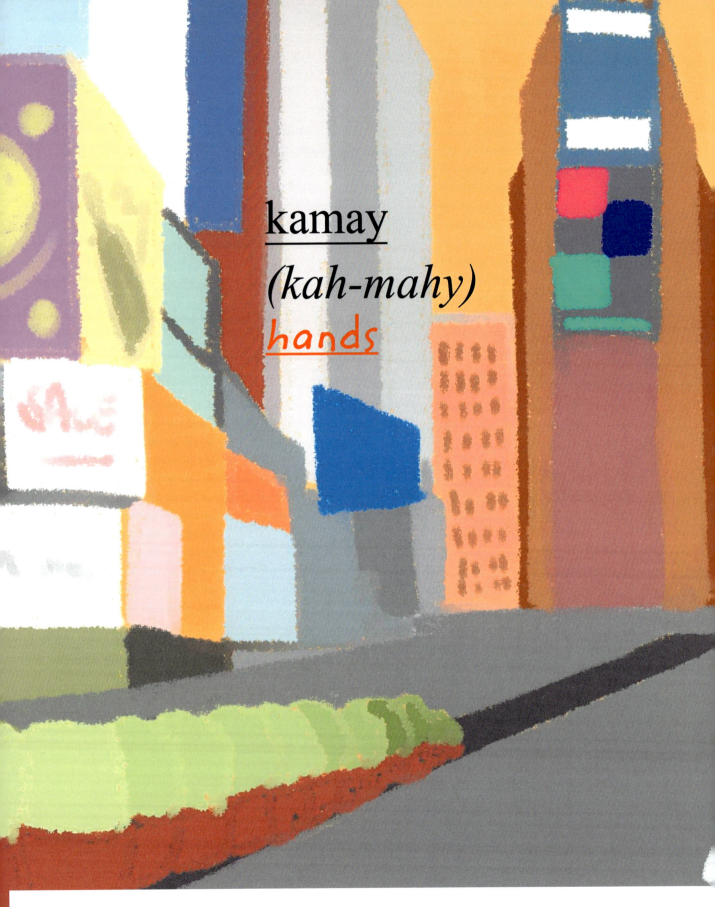

kamay

*(kah-mahy)*

*hands*

Times Square

Central Park

at <u>paa</u>

*(aht pah-ah)*

and <u>feet</u>

# dalawang <u>mata</u>
## *(dah-lah-wahng mah-tah)*
two <u>eyes</u>

Rockefeller Center observatory dock

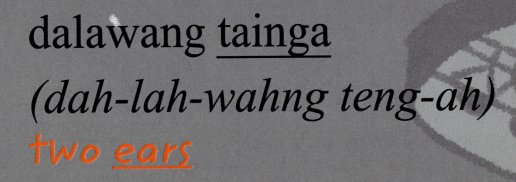

dalawang <u>tainga</u>

*(dah-lah-wahng teng-ah)*

two <u>ears</u>

Madison Square Garden

ilong na maganda

(*ee-long nah mah-gahn-dah*)

nose is beautiful

Brooklyn Bridge

maliliit na ngipin

*(mah-lee-lee-eet nah ngee-pin)*

little teeth

NYC subway

NYC restaurant

masarap kumain

*(mah-sah-rahp koo-mah-in)*

delicious eating

Grand Central Station

dilang maliit nag sasabi
(dee-lahng mah-lee-it nahg
sah-sah-bee)
little tongue that says

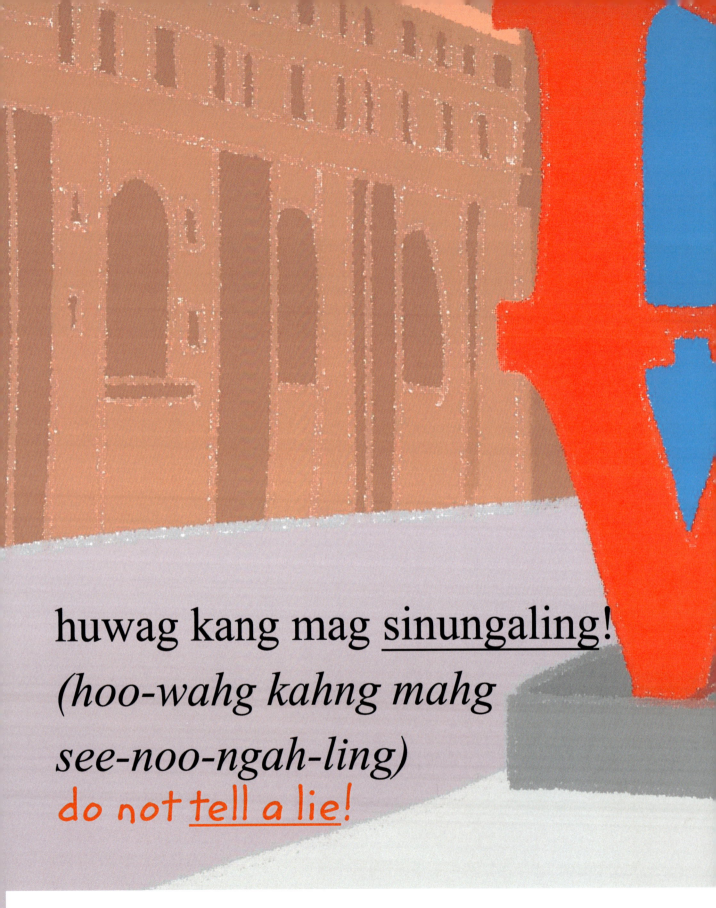

huwag kang mag <u>sinungaling</u>!
*(hoo-wahg kahng mahg*

*see-noo-ngah-ling)*
do not <u>tell a lie</u>!

'Love' sculpture

# Sampung Mga Daliri

Traditional Filipino folk song

## Tagalog Version

Sampung mga daliri
kamay
at paa
dalawang mata
dalawang tainga
ilong na maganda
maliliit na ngipin
masarap kumain
dilang maliit nag sasabi
huwag kang mag sinungaling


## English Version

Ten little fingers
hands
and feet
two eyes
two ears
nose is beautiful
little teeth
delicious eating
little tongue that says
do not tell a lie

## About the Author

Adriana is a Filipina and moved to New York City, United States when she was three years old. She is mom to two children whom the books are dedicated to. She looked for books on Filipino-American culture and couldn't find any so she decided to write them herself for her children.

## About the Illustrator

Raquel is a self-taught freelance illustrator based in the Philippines. She graduated BSN with honors but realized that her true passion lies in bringing words to life through illustrations. She is mostly interested in creating picture books and designing cute characters though digital media.

Made in the USA
Middletown, DE
30 January 2019